CONNECTING WITH KIDS

IN A DISCONNECTED WORLD

CONNECTING WITH KIDS
IN A DISCONNECTED WORLD

Trevor Romain

Connecting With Kids In A Disconnected World

Published by The Trevor Romain Company
Austin, TX
www.trevorromain.com

ISBN: 978-1-64339-995-9

Printed in the United States of America

CONTENTS

CONNECTING WITH KIDS

IN A DISCONNECTED WORLD

The truth is, rarely can a response
make something better — what makes
something better is a connection.

—Brené Brown

INTRODUCTION

I am not a parent of biological children, but I have been a stepdad, a substitute dad, a reserve dad, a fill-in dad, and the proud father of an imaginary child.

I have not nurtured kids of my own, but I have worked with terminally ill kids, refugee kids, foster kids, military kids, traumatized kids, at-risk kids, struggling cartoon kids, and orphans.

Over the last twenty-five years, I have seen over forty kids through end of life, worked with former child soldiers in Central Africa, volunteered at orphanages, and worked with US military kids who are constantly on the move and whose parents are struggling with PTSD, have committed suicide, or are deployed.

Over the years, I have learned to connect with kids

even under the most trying circumstances. This book is a collection of my journal entries, observations, anecdotes, sketches, screwups, poignant memories, life-changing moments, and the tough lessons I have learned while working with kids.

HOW CHILDREN WITH CANCER TAUGHT ME HOW TO CONNECT WITH KIDS

I have been asked many times over the years if there was an initial "aha" moment that sparked my connection with kids.

The answer is yes. There were actually a few situations, but one stands out in particular.

It happened many years ago after I wrote and illustrated a children's book called *The Keeper of the Dreams*. It was a picture book about a little girl who loses her dreams and has to face her biggest fear, the Bogey Man, to get them back.

I decided that I wanted to donate the book to a charity, so I offered it to a number of local non-profits in Austin where I live, but nobody was really interested in the project.

A few months later, I presented the book to a non-profit for kids with cancer called the Candlelighters Childhood Cancer Foundation, now named the American Childhood Cancer Organization.

With the help of supporters, the book was published, and we were able to raise a decent sum of money for the organization.

A few months later, one of the board members of the organization said to me, "You wrote a book to help kids with cancer, but have you ever met one?"

I shook my head.

"Well, she said, "I think it's about time."

I agreed, and she organized a book reading in the oncology wing at our local children's hospital.

I must admit, I was extremely nervous when I walked into the hospital. I was taken upstairs to a small playroom, and inside, waiting for me, were about sixteen kids of various ages. All of them were dressed in hospital gowns, bald from chemotherapy, and attached to IV poles.

I felt so uneasy and sorry for those kids that I wanted

to run out of the place. The only thing to do was to read the book to them immediately. I introduced myself and began reading.

The kids listened with rapture.

After the story was over, I closed the book and smiled. A little girl of six suddenly put up her hand.

"Can you read it again?" she asked earnestly.

"Sure," I replied and read the book again.

Well, it turns out that I read the book at least five times that day because, every time I thought I was done, another kid would ask me to read it again.

Reading the book connected me to the kids in an indescribable way, and I stayed to chat and joke with them for a couple of hours.

As I was leaving, a little boy named Alex put up his hand and said, "Are you coming back tomorrow?"

For some reason, without hesitation, I said, "Yes."

I went back for over twenty years. They called me "the Doctor of Mischief" and even gave me a lab coat with my name embroidered on it.

I still visit kids in hospitals across the world when I get the chance.

Kids with cancer have taught me the value of life,

the importance of living in the now, and how to connect with others even in the most adverse and traumatic of situations. I can honestly say I would not be doing what I do today if it were not for reading the book that day. One little children's book, sixteen very sick children, and those two hours changed my life completely.

It started me on a journey of connecting with kids and launched me on an incredible path that I still walk almost twenty-five years later.

I'm proud to say that I became a board member of the local Candlelighters chapter. Then, for fifteen years, I served as board member of the American Childhood Cancer Organization, where, for a two-year period, I was also board president.

The most important thing in communication is to hear what isn't being said.

—Peter Drucker

HOW MY FATHER CONNECTED WITH ME

I was very lucky as a child that my father devised a wonderful plan to help the two of us connect. I had no idea at the time that it was all planned, but it worked.

On Tuesdays, in the late afternoon, he would take me out for hot chocolate and a chat. (My brother had the Wednesday afternoon slot.)

During our time together, my dad would normally start talking about things he was working through. He sometimes talked about his own failures or struggles. I remember on one occasion he apologized for an argument he'd had with my mom in front of us kids.

Another time, when he got a bonus at work, he asked me if I thought we should use the money to fix up our playroom or use it for a vacation.

His actions created such a trust in him that when he cleverly and nonchalantly asked me what was going on in my life, I told him everything. Yes, everything, even the shameful and embarrassing stuff.

I shared everything that was going on in my life with my dad until the day he died.

TOO MUCH SCREEN TIME CAN CAUSE DEPRESSION AND LOSS OF EMOTIONAL CONNECTION

In their book *Cyberbullying in Social Media Within Educational Institutions* (2015), authors Merle Horowitz and Dorothy M. Bollinger summarize the results of a clinical report on the negative impact of social media on children:

Researchers have proposed a new phenomenon called "Facebook depression," defined as depression that develops when preteens and teens spend a great deal of time on social media sites, such as Facebook, and then begin to exhibit classic symptoms of depression. … The intensity of the online world is thought to be a factor that may trigger depression in some adolescents. As with offline depression, preadolescents and adolescents who suffer from Facebook depression are at risk for social isolation and sometimes turn to risky Internet sites and blogs for "help" that may promote substance abuse, unsafe sexual practices, or aggressive or self-destructive behaviors.

According to British market researcher Childwise, kids aged five to sixteen spend an average of six and a half hours a day in front of a screen.

Research shows that connections between adults and kids are decaying rapidly due to electronic devices. A Kaiser Family Foundation study estimated that kids over sixteen spend an average of nine hours a day on social media.

An AC Nielson study has shown that the average American watches more than five hours of television a day. Over the year, that's more than two months of non-stop television. In a sixty-five-year life, that person would have spent over nine years watching TV.

CONNECTING DOS AND DON'TS

Do slow down and listen without trying to answer for children. Let them finish what they are trying to say.

Don't go over the top with positive reactions. Overenthusiasm is often interpreted as fake by kids and tends to shut down communication instead of fostering it.

Don't ignore the superficial, because triviality will often lead to what is really on the child's mind.

Don't be an interrogator. Be a person.

Do share your own deep feelings. This will show the child that it is safe to go below the surface.

Don't speak with a higher-pitched, childlike voice. It makes children uncomfortable.

Do pay attention to the child's conversational style:

Remember, some kids don't like questions. Others communicate better with prompts. Many take time to warm up to conversation.

WE OFTEN TELL KIDS WHAT WE THINK THEY NEED TO HEAR...

I had an experience that highlighted this in Bujumbura, Burundi, during a trip I took with the United Nations to work with children in refugee camps and orphanages.

As we got out of our vehicle in the compound, we were rushed by a number of kids. They grabbed our arms and held our hands excitedly.

A few minutes later, one of the workers came along with a rolled-up newspaper and swatted at the kids to disperse them. They all scattered except for one little boy, who, cleverly, put his finger through my belt loop and stubbornly hung on.

The worker tried to dislodge the boy with a tap on the head with the paper, but I told him it was okay to let the boy stay. He hung onto my belt loop all morning.

INSTEAD OF LISTENING TO WHAT THEY ARE ASKING FOR.

A little later, the boy tugged on my sleeve and wanted to ask me a question. In broken English, and with the help of a translator, I told the boy to go ahead.

"Can you help me find my mommy?" he asked sincerely.

Before I could answer, one of the workers patted the boy on the head and said, "I told you, we are going to find all your mommies one day."

I immediately put up my hand and told the worker to stop. What he was selling the kid was a bold-faced lie. None of those kids had mothers.

I kneeled down, getting eye to eye with the little boy.

"Where do you think your mommy is?" I asked in a soft voice.

"She's in heaven," said the boy, pointing upward.

"Ahhh," I replied. "You know what? Tonight, when I say my prayers, I'm going to pass on a message to your mom to tell her that you love her and miss her and will never forget her, okay?"

The boy threw his arms around my neck and hugged me.

"Thank you, mister," he said and ran off to join the other kids, who were playing soccer with a rolled-up bundle of cloth that they were using as a ball.

All that little boy needed was validation and someone to hear what he was asking for instead of trying to fix how he felt by appeasing him.

DISCOUNTING A CHILD'S FEELINGS IS THE QUICKEST WAY TO DISCONNECT FROM THEM

"Don't worry" or "Don't be afraid," followed by "It's going to be okay," will not help a child stop worrying or cease being scared. All it does is help adults deal with their own discomfort around the child's situation.

Shutting kids down by telling them not to feel something negates their feelings and pushes them away instead of making a connection with them.

Telling a child not to worry simply blocks the child's feelings and leaves them disconnected so they have to deal with their stresses alone, causing them to become swamped by their own emotions.

Kneeling down to the child's level, making eye contact, and even tilting your head shows the child that you are focusing on and listening to what they are telling you.

Every kid has a sign on his or her head that says, "Make me special."

USING ART TO COMMUNICATE

Creating art is an effective way to help kids express and process difficult feelings.

Arts and crafts help kids develop self-confidence.

Expressing visual art is a powerful form of non-verbal communication for kids. It's extremely helpful for children who are unable to articulate their thoughts, sensations, emotions, or perceptions with words.

Research has shown that some of the sensory characteristics of making art are particularly effective in improving a child's moods and their sense of well-being.

The process of making art has been proven to calm both the mind and the body, especially for children who have experienced trauma in their lives, such as divorce, loss of a loved one, moving, and bullying.

HOW A DRAWING HELPED ME CONNECT WITH A TERMINALLY ILL CHILD

Drawing, painting, crafts, and even simple doodling are powerful connectors in my box of communicational tools.

I often just sit down with kids and invite them to draw with me. At first, they are reluctant, so I don't force them to participate. I just place pen and paper nearby, and I start doing simple doodles. You don't have to be an artist to make this approach work. It's amazing how kids will watch an adult draw, even if it's only stick figures. Most of the time, kids will pick up the pencil or marker that I left nearby and start drawing their own picture.

On occasion, I will start a stick figure drawing and

invite the child to complete it.

If the child is reluctant to draw, I often challenge them to see who can do the worst drawing.

One of my biggest connection breakthroughs with a child happened through a simple drawing. I was volunteering at the oncology ward at our local children's hospital. One afternoon, I went to visit a young ten-year-old named Victor, who was putting up an incredible fight after a harrowing bone marrow transplant.

We were drawing together in his hospital room when he suddenly turned to me and said, "What's going to happen to me when I die?"

Before I could say a word, his mom ran over to the bed and said, "You are not going to die, okay? I don't know how many times I have to tell you."

Behind his mother's back, the kid looked at me, shrugged, pulled a tongue, and flashed a broad, mischievous smile.

A short while later, his mom left the room, and I said to him, "You know, buddy, we're all going to die one day..."

"I know," he said, interrupting me. "She thinks

I'm stupid. I know what's going on. Hey, do you think there's...like...a heaven up there?"

"I hope so," I said, taken aback by his question.

"Do you think they give you a map when you get there?" he said.

"Huh?"

"The place must be huge," he said, "How do you know where to go?"

I laughed so hard I about sprayed the coffee I was drinking out of my nose.

"I'll tell you what," I said. "If you die from this disease while you're still a kid, ask for my grandpa when you get up there. His name is Ted Tanchel."

"What do you mean?" he said, laughing.

I told him all about my late grandfather and what a wonderful, caring man he was and hopefully still is.

"Look for him when you get up there. He'll get you checked in and get you a great room," I said.

"But how will I find him?" he asked. "There must be, like, millions of people up there."

I thought for a moment and then pictured my grandfather. In my mind, I saw his face as clear as daylight.

"Hang on," I said, and I drew a quick picture of my grandpa in my journal. I tore out the page and gave it to him. "Remember, his name is Ted Tanchel. Memorize that picture."

He looked at the drawing of my grandpa and said, "He looks real nice."

"Oh, he's the best," I said, putting my hand on my heart. "You'll see."

The next time I came to visit Victor, the picture of my grandfather was up on the corkboard in his room, next to all his get-well cards.

When I teased him, as I often did, he would point to the picture of my grandfather and tell me he was going to tell my grandpa about it when he saw him, if I didn't stop.

I'm very sad to say that cancer won the battle and Victor died about five months later.

His mom asked me to deliver the eulogy at his funeral. It was one of the hardest things I have ever done in my life.

I went to the church only to discover that it was an open-casket ceremony. I had never seen a child in a coffin before, and I did not want to see him like that, so I avoided the casket and went into the church. They wheeled the bloody coffin into the church and put it next to the pulpit. Open!

The priest delivered his sermon and then called me up to do the eulogy. I did a humorous memorial based on Victor's wicked sense of humor. I wanted to celebrate his life instead of mourning his death.

We all laughed so hard, and I managed not to look at the coffin the whole time.

As I finished my speech, I pointed to the coffin and said, "As he was dying, that little boy taught me so much about living…" As I spoke, I accidentally glanced at the coffin.

I'm so glad I did.

Victor was lying there with his hands resting on his chest. He looked so comfortable and at peace. He was dressed in a black tuxedo with a red bow tie. His head was bald from the chemotherapy. He had such a sweet, innocent, peaceful look on his face.

In his coffin, surrounding his body, were all his childhood toys. And a sea of flowers.

I smiled and mouthed goodbye to him as I walked past the coffin on the way back to my seat.

That's when I saw the picture of my grandfather that he was holding in his hand.

It was a simple, silly drawing of my grandfather, but the picture itself wasn't important. What was important was how a pencil and a scrap of paper created a connection between us that helped form an amazing bond and months of important and meaningful interactions.

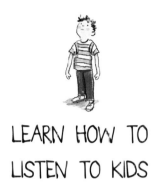

LEARN HOW TO
LISTEN TO KIDS

Let kids know you are listening, especially if they are talking about their worries and concerns.

Hear what they are saying, even if it is tough to listen to.

Express interest in what they are saying instead of being intrusive.

Let them finish what they are saying before you jump in with a response.

Repeat back what you heard to make sure you understand what they were sharing.

Reflecting statements back to kids acknowledges and gives words to their feelings.

HOW A POSITIVE CONNECTION WITH ONE TEACHER CHANGED MY SCHOOL EXPERIENCE

I battled at school mainly because I am somewhat dyslexic and I struggle with ADD. I had a great connection with my ninth-grade English teacher, Mr. Paul Clingman, who was also a musician. I struggled with English all through school and failed the subject many times. I just couldn't feel it, especially essay writing, until he suggested I write a poem instead of an essay for one of our homework assignments.

That simple suggestion changed everything for me. I loved and enjoyed writing that poem. I became obsessed with poetry. That, in turn, led me to love English, and believe it or not, I developed an affinity for essay writing.

Mr. Clingman's class was the first time I ever got an A in high school. The connection I had with him motivated me more than any of the reprimands, corporal punishment, and detentions I got for failing English.

Connecting with Mr. Clingman was the catalyst that set me on the road to being a writer. Despite my struggles at school, the connection with him led me to a writing career with a number of best-selling children's books and over a million copies in print in twenty-two different languages. Thank you, Mr. Clingman, for bending the rules a little to connect with me so the light could come through.

ONE VERY SIMPLE WAY TO CONNECT WITH KIDS

When kids are going through stress or a tough time, they often withdraw and internalize their feelings. They present themselves as doing fine when it is obvious to an adult that something is amiss.

The inability at that moment for the child to express what they are really feeling creates a void between adult and child.

The same can be said for adults who pretend everything is okay when kids know that it is not.

During these stressful times, connections and communication between adults and children often become uncomfortable or break down completely.

I came up with a plan to help a teacher friend of mine who was going through a rough patch with one of his students. I suggested they each have a box into which they could post notes to each other.

Next to each box, he placed a blank pile of cards and a pen.

The plan worked.

The boy became more and more open with each note, and pretty soon, the contents of the notes became the seeds of very important conversations and teaching moments for my friend.

DISCONNECTION THROUGH FEAR OF INTIMACY

One out of every five adults fears intimacy and closeness in Western cultures.

Children who are at the receiving end of someone who fears being connected may feel dismissed and completely rejected. This can cause frustration, sadness, and emptiness for the child.

All children have a natural need to be nurtured by adults so they can receive protection and comfort when they are under stress. How an adult responds can have a major impact on a child's development.

Sometimes, when adults are emotionally detached or distressed, children cannot express themselves without fear of triggering a negative response in the adults, so they keep quiet and suffer alone.

I had a firsthand experience of negative responses brought on by the fear of intimacy during a visit to a school on a US military base a few years ago.

After my presentation, a young girl who was about nine years old approached me. She told me that her father was deployed and that her mother had grown very distant while her dad was away.

She told me that her mom would tell her to watch television or play and then would lock herself in her bedroom.

The little girl said that she would then creep out of her room and sit by her mother's door and rock.

When she heard her mother getting off the bed, the girl told me she would rush back to her room and busy herself so that her mother never knew about her sitting at the door. She told me she didn't want to tell her mother because she was afraid it would upset her mother more than she already was.

Unfortunately, due to a lack of connection during this traumatic time, the girl had to carry her mother's pain and the worry about her father being gone all by herself.

Chronic loneliness can be brought on by trauma or emotional neglect. (Trauma can be caused by bullying, divorce, military deployment, relocation, etc.) A child may be in a position where everything seems normal on the outside but still feels lonely and cannot thrive if they can't get the love and attention they need from a parent or caregiver.

A withdrawn parent or caregiver is not likely to be emotionally available to the child, which leaves the child feeling stranded and alone.

The telling and hearing of stories is a bonding ritual that breaks through illusions of separateness and activates a deep sense of our collective interdependence.

—Annette Simmons

DID YOU KNOW THAT SHARING STORIES WITH KIDS CAN ACTUALLY IMPROVE THEIR SELF-ESTEEM AND HELP THEM DEAL WITH STRESS?

A study conducted at Emory University found that the more children had been told stories about their family history, the higher their self-esteem and the better able they were to deal with the effects of stress.

"Family stories provide a sense of identity through time, and help children understand who they are in the world," the researchers said in their paper.

Stories are the foundation of memory and learning. They connect the past, present, and future by giving us real-life examples so we can learn to anticipate the possible consequences of our actions.

HOW AN OLD MAN, A CRASHED BICYCLE, DISRESPECTFUL TEENS, AND A SIMPLE STORY HAVE KEPT ME CONNECTED TO THOUSANDS OF KIDS

Sharing my personal stories with young people has not only helped me connect with them but helped me inspire them too.

My favorite story is a simple one, but it has connected me to thousands and thousands of children who not only felt a bond after they heard it but were moved to make a positive contribution to the world.

The story took place a long time ago, when people actually did what they said they were going to do.

I was driving along a dirt road in the Drakensberg

Mountains in South Africa with my girlfriend.

In the distance, I noticed a speck on the horizon, a speck that would teach me something that, until then, I did not know even existed.

Integrity.

I know it's a big word and hard to explain, but I will try nonetheless.

You see, that speck on the horizon was a very old, toothless African man with a white beard riding an old bicycle.

I slowed down so that I didn't spew dust all over the poor old guy.

I waved at him, and he waved back as we passed. His smile was wonderfully warm and friendly. He looked about eighty and way too old to be driving a bicycle.

I watched him in my rear-view and then looked up to see a pickup truck coming toward me at full speed. It was moving very quickly. There was a dust cloud billowing behind it.

As the truck passed me, I saw three young guys in the front seat. One of them had a beer in his hand.

I glanced at my rear-view, and my heart almost stopped. The driver of the pickup truck was heading straight for the old man on the bicycle. I saw the old guy look nervously over his shoulder as the vehicle came up from behind.

I closed my eyes because I knew that they were going to try and dislodge him from his bicycle.

I opened my eyes and saw them swerving towards him, missing him by inches. I could also see them gesticulating and shouting at the man as they drove past.

The old man wobbled on that bike, and I saw him drive off the road and crash down a little ditch.

I slowed down and turned the car around.

I got to the old man, and he was sitting down in the veld, rubbing his knee. The front wheel of his bike was buckled and bent.

The old man looked so sad. "Haai eh-eh," he said, shaking his head. "What is wrong with those kids?"

"Are you okay?" I asked.

"I am," he replied. "It is just my heart that is sore."

He told us he was a gardener at the Champaign Castle Hotel and was on his way to work.

I put his bicycle in the trunk of the car, and we took him to the hotel, which was about three or four miles away. Apparently, he drove his rattletrap bike to work every day, rain or shine.

As we were leaving, I gave the man about forty rand in cash that I had in my wallet and a few rand my girlfriend had in her purse. "It's to fix your bike," I said.

"I'm so sorry," he said, "I can't take your money."

My girlfriend told him to take the money because I was just going to use it to buy drinks and get drunk anyway.

The old man chuckled and told me I had a wise girlfriend.

"I will pay you back," he said, smiling sincerely.

"That's okay," I said. "You don't have to."

But he insisted that I give him my address, and I did so on a little scrap of paper, knowing that he would lose it in about ten seconds.

Needless to say, I had the resources to find more beer money. My girlfriend and I had a great weekend in the mountains, and I forgot about the old man.

The scuffed and wrinkled white envelope arrived at my little flat in Sandringham, Johannesburg, one month later.

In it was a one-rand note! (This was about a dollar in those days.)

Yes, the old man had done what he'd said he was going to do.

I swear, at the end of every month, an envelope arrived with a one-rand note in it. No letter, no return address, just the money the old man had promised to pay me back.

I was in advertising in those days, and a little over a year later, I went back to the Drakensberg to shoot another television commercial.

The filming took place very close to where that old man had fallen off his bike, and I decided to go and find him and tell him he didn't need to send me the money every month because I was doing fine.

I found out that he had retired from the hotel. They told me that he lived in the village near where I had first seen him, and they told me where his place was.

My art director and I went to his home. It was exactly what you'd imagine: a thatched mud hut with the holes of missing windowpanes covered in SPAR plastic shopping bags to keep the wind out.

An old African granny with gray hair answered the door. She had a doek (scarf) on her head that was tied under her chin like people used to do in the olden days when they had a toothache.

Inside the hut, the floor was hardened mud and swept clean. There was a gas stovetop, a galvanized tub with a bar of Sunlight soap in it, a rickety old table with a clean cloth on it, a little cupboard, and a bed with white sheets on bricks.

That's all. It was spotless.

The bar of Sunlight soap was the only thing of color in the entire place. I have such a clear vision of that bar of soap. I can see it in my mind when I close my eyes.

Other than those few items, the place was spare. The woman was the old man's wife. I asked if he was around so I could tell him that he didn't have to pay the money back to me. What she told me stopped me cold.

The old man had died six months before, and she had continued paying his debt. I was stunned. She had nothing. Absolutely NOTHING! Yet she was doing what she considered was the right thing: paying their debt back as promised. She had kept his word, sending me money every month despite the fact that her husband had died and she was dirt poor.

I told her I didn't need the money, and I gave her a little more that I had in my pocket.

She was so grateful and would not stop hugging me.

As we walked away from the old man's home, I turned and saw his bicycle leaning against the side of the hut.

Stories help kids understand their own fears, emotions, and feelings. Some stories, like that of the old man and the bicycle, introduce ethics and values and expand children's understanding of the world so they can better connect with the people in it. Sharing stories gives children a wide range of possibilities upon which to draw when dealing with life events.

Nothing is more exciting and bonding in a relationship than creating together.

—Stephen Covey

THE BENEFITS OF SHARING PERSONAL STORIES WITH KIDS

Instills morals, values, and virtues in children.

Helps kids improve verbal proficiency.

Improves listening skills.

Encourages creativity and imagination.

Helps improve memory.

Fosters better communication.

Helps children better understand difficult situations.

Reduces screen time.

USING OBJECTS TO CONNECT WITH KIDS

To keep me occupied while logging thousands of miles on airplanes as I travel from place to place to share stories, I often doodle on stones. I call them "Hope ROCKS!"

The rocks are actually objects I use to connect with kids. These are known as transitional objects in the psychology world.

For example, I used one of these rocks during a school tour to Germany a few years ago. At the school, I met a little girl whose parents were going through a divorce. She was distraught and sobbing so hard while trying to tell me how she was feeling.

I happened to have one of my hope rocks in my pocket, and I gave it to her. I told her that whenever she felt sad, anxious, or lonely to hold it in her hand and know there was someone with her all the way

A smile tickled her mouth, and she threw her arms around me and thanked me for the rock. Her teacher had to pry her arms away. "Thanks for the stone," she said as the teacher led her back to her classroom. "I'll keep it forever."

Eight months later, we were at another school at a different base in Germany. After my performance, I saw a teacher standing nearby with her class. She suddenly put her hand to her mouth and pointed at me. She was sobbing.

Then I saw a blur out of the corner of my eye. Before I knew what was happening, I was almost knocked off my feet by a child running up and hugging me. She looked up, and I recognized her immediately. It was the same girl I had given the stone to eight months before. She had moved and was now at a different school on another base.

She was sobbing but smiling at the same time. "I'm so happy to see you," I said.

"Me too," she said. "My daddy is deployed. But look." She reached into her pocket and brought out a crumpled and frayed Kleenex. She unraveled it, and inside was the stone I had given her all those months before. The doodles were practically worn off the sides.

"You kept it?" I said, smiling. "You made my day."

Her teacher, who was standing nearby, still in tears, said, "She carries that stone with her every single day."

"My dad is deployed right now, and the stone gives me hope," she said.

I looked over at my business partner, Woody Englander, who was standing nearby. He started to cry. So did I.

The little girl carefully wrapped the rock in the Kleenex and put it back into her pocket. Then she noticed me wiping my tears.

She stepped forward and gave me a giant hug.

"It's okay," she said, patting my back while hugging me. "It's okay."

Nothing can grow in your comfort zone.

DISCOMFORT DOES NOT HAVE TO LEAD TO DISCONNECTION

One of my most powerful connections with a child occurred when I was at my most uncomfortable.

It happened during a school assembly: I met Juliana Wetmore. Juliana is one in a billion. She is one of four or five of people in the world born without a face. (Her new adopted sister also suffers from Treacher Collins, the same syndrome.)

Juliana has had countless surgeries to start creating a face that will take many years and many, many more operations as she grows. She is hearing impaired, breathes through a trach tube, and, at present, eats through a feeding tube (although, apparently, she has started to lick cheese off a pretzel stick). She was featured in a documentary called *Born Without A Face* not too long ago.

One of the most amazing things about Juliana is that she goes to a REGULAR school and is actually a grade ahead of most of her classmates in academics. She is extremely smart, warm, friendly, and, well, just a regular kid.

We met Juliana because she happened to be with her third-grade class during one of my performances at her school in Jacksonville, Florida, on our USO world tour. (Juliana's dad is in the navy.)

It was very hard at first for my mind to actually process what I was seeing. It was heart-stopping, to say the least. I was stunned when I first saw her, but boy, did that little golden soul of hers shine out of those sweet eyes and through those Coke-bottle glasses in no time. To see her chuckling at my dumb jokes and giving me a thumbs up after my story about Botshabelo orphanage in South Africa stands as one of the most powerful experiences I have ever had.

I fell in love with her instantly.

She was the first person to ask me a question during

the Q&A section, and she came up and gave me the biggest hug when I was done with my presentation.

She stood next to me while I was talking to another young girl who had recently lost a family member. While I was speaking to the tearful little girl, Juliana slipped her hand into mine and stood alongside me, patiently holding my fingers while I listened to her grieving friend.

Then, after another hug and a little wave, she left the cafeteria with her class.

HOW BOOKS CAN CONNECT FAMILIES

Create a family book club. Read what kids are reading so you can discuss and share ideas about the books.

Mutual love for books and meaningful discussions helps to create a connection between readers.

I'll never forget the day I discovered the magic of books. I was in primary school, and my grade-two teacher, Mrs. Varrie, started reading to us from a book about the Secret Seven by Enid Blyton. I was intrigued. I could not believe such an exciting story was coming out of two pieces of cardboard with pages in it.

At the end of the school day, I milled around until my teacher left the classroom, and I picked up the book. I was a slow beginner reader, so books did not particularly appeal to me until that day.

I thumbed through the book and looked at all those words. I touched the pages, ran my fingers along the slightly raised typography, and even turned the book upside down. I think I was trying to shake the story out of the book. I could not fathom how such a compelling story was living in that jumble of letters. It was astounding that all those words, lines, and paragraphs contained tales that appeared as movies so clearly in my mind.

I could not wait to get home after school to ask my mom to get me a Secret Seven book. She did a few days later, but it was a little too difficult for me to read by myself, so my dad read it to me.

However, the next night, as I was sitting in bed, my mom came into the room and handed me another book. It was the original *Winnie-the-Pooh*, with drawings by E.H. Shepard. (It had a similar illustration style to the picture above, not the Disney version that you now see.) I can still see the blue cover in my mind's eye. I opened the book and began to read...

"Here is Edward Bear, coming downstairs now, bump, bump, bump, on the back of his head, behind

Christopher Robin. It is, as far as he knows, the only way of coming downstairs, but sometimes he feels that there really is another way, if only he could stop bumping for a moment and think of it. And then he feels that perhaps there isn't."

There and then...my world changed.

I stayed connected to Mrs. Varrie for over forty years until she died. Even as an adult, I would speak to Mrs. Varrie from across the world to discuss books and writing.

Reading has the power to bring out the best in us. Sharing books can forge links and connect individuals who might otherwise appear to have little in common.

MAKE A POWERFUL CONNECTION BY SIMPLY TAPPING INTO THINGS THAT A CHILD IS PASSIONATE ABOUT

Twelve-year-old Vicki was absolutely stunning. Even though she was hounded by cancer and tormented by chemotherapy, she still radiated beauty.

Vicki was passionate about being a model. That's mostly what we talked about. We often discussed modeling and acting. I had been an advertising creative director in a previous life, before becoming a writer, so I had great stories to share with her. Sharing and discussing her passion helped us form a wonderful bond.

I knew she was close to the end of her life, though, and being a model was one dream that would probably not come true for her.

Or could it?

I called my friend Randal (a wonderful photographer) and asked him if he would help.

He certainly did.

We brought the photographic equipment to the hospital and turned Vicki's room into a real photography studio. There were wires and lights and cameras and reflectors and people all over the room.

That afternoon, we took a series of memorable pictures. It was a truly amazing experience.

Here was a child, hooked up to machines, totally nauseated from chemotherapy, and still running the show, making sure that nothing in the world was going to take the moment from her.

In the middle of the photo session, a nurse came in to give Vicki a round of medicine. The picture taking was interrupted while Vicki was about to be medicated through a tube that went directly into her heart. The nurse wasn't very happy that day, and her attitude reflected it.

She was downright snitty, to tell the truth, and rather put out by the goings on in the room. As the nurse was about to walk over to the bed, Vicki looked up and very calmly said, "Err, excuse me. Do you mind leaving your bad mood outside?"

Vicki's mom, Liz, and I laughed so hard we almost collapsed. Even the nurse burst out laughing.

Sometimes, when I feel grumpy or a bit down and find myself taking it out on other people, I think of Vicki. She had every right in the world to be miserable and depressed, but she always found time to smile, joke, and make the most of her situation. She lived every moment fully. Even doctors from the other units would pop in to visit her when they needed a pick-me-up.

After the photo shoot, I said to Vicki, "Girl. You were great! Your dream of becoming a model came true. I hope thousands of people will get to see your picture."

"Then I'll be one of those people who only becomes famous after they're dead," she said, grinning. (Vicki had a wicked sense of humor.)

"You'll be famous."

"Promise?" she said, imitating the pout of a spoiled model.

"Oh yeah. You will."

A number of weeks later, the glint in her beautiful

blue eyes started to fade, and hope (along with her inimitable spirit) slowly drifted like a skyward balloon from her body.

She died peacefully with her favorite people holding her.

I kept my promise and made Vicki famous many years later by publishing her story and the photograph on multiple social media sites, garnering many thousands of likes and shares.

The photo, which I still have, connected us then and has kept us connected for over twenty years even though she passed away so long ago.

Volunteering and community service with kids creates stronger bonds. It helps form closer relationships, better connections, and more powerful attachments.

Doing community service with kids is a very powerful and meaningful way to connect with them. I saw a perfect example of this in South Africa during one of my trips there.

While there, I went to the cemetery where my grandfather is buried, in a little town called Parys in the Orange Free State. My grandfather was a farmer in a nearby town called Vredefort.

The tombstones lie in a clearing surrounded by blue gum eucalyptus trees, thorn bushes, and yellow savannah grass. The cemetery is no longer in use, and when we got there, sadly, we found the outside overgrown.

Most of the families who have kin buried there have passed away or moved on to bigger cities two or three hours away like my mother did.

I opened the rusty gate, and we walked through the tall, dry grass to where my grandfather rests.

As we made our way into the clearing, sitting between two gravestones, we noticed an African man on an overturned plastic paint bucket with his back to us. He was washing one of the tombstones with a cloth.

In front of him were three barefoot little African kids. Two girls and a boy. They were sweeping around the graves with brooms that were made of dried grass. It was so sweet. They were happily chatting away while they swept. They could not have been more than five or six years old.

It was too cute how seriously they were taking their chore.

The kids suddenly stopped sweeping when they saw

us and looked a little afraid. The man turned, saw us, and stood up. He wiped his hands on his faded pants.

"Morning, ma'am. Good morning, sir," he said, touching the brim of his hat with his finger.

"Good morning," we replied.

The man said something to the kids in what I believe was Tswana. The kids backed away and started moving off.

"No, don't worry," I said, smiling. "It's no problem. The kids are doing an important job."

"Very important," said the man, smiling back.

I waved at the kids and said hello.

The man said something to the kids in his language, and they waved back at us.

"Hello," they all said, grinning broadly.

"That is my grandfather's grave," I said, pointing to a gravestone near the kids. "And over there is my great-grandfather and great-grandmother."

"Ma'am, is that your father?" he said, pointing at my grandfather's grave.

"Yes it is," said my mom in her sweet, high voice as the kids looked on very inquisitively.

"Mmm, mmm, mmm," he said, nodding. "Don't

worry, ma'am, I always look after your daddy and his friends very nicely."

I marveled at the connection and the bond between the old man and the kids, realizing afterward that the volunteer community service they performed together connected them in a special and meaningful way.

When we were ready to leave, I asked the man who was responsible for paying him to maintain the cemetery, as I wanted to contribute.

He told me nobody was paying him. He said he just came to the cemetery every couple of weeks with his grandchildren and did some cleaning up. He said he was passing by one day and saw that the graves were overgrown and some were even falling over and he just wanted to make it nice.

"You should get paid," I said. "And I'm happy to do so. It's a very big job, looking after this place."

"Oh, It's not a job, sir," he said, looking around at the graves. "It's just respect."

FOR A BETTER CONNECTION WITH KIDS, TURN NEGATIVE TALK INTO POSITIVE

Adults are sometimes surprised when kids don't do what they are told to do. What they don't realize is that demand phrases like "Put your toys away now!" or "This room is disgusting!" are often interpreted as negative and sometimes hurtful talk, for obvious reasons. The continued use of this style of communication can also turn into perceived nagging and become counterproductive. Simply turn the phrase into positive talk for better results, saying things like, "Let's get this place cleaned up so we can enjoy our dinner," or, "Let's put the toys away so we can have some fun getting ready for school."

CONNECTING WITHOUT WORDS

Some of my most effective and meaningful connections have been wordless.

One of the most memorable occurred in my youth. As a little boy, I often stood on the chair behind my dad with my arms lovingly wrapped around his neck as he sketched or layered colors onto his pen and ink drawings.

I loved being with him in his studio. He never told me to go away. Not once. I would stand there for hours, draped over his shoulders, watching him as he painted. Every so often, he would put down his brush and nuzzle my neck with his face. Then he would pick up the brush and continue painting.

The beautiful, dance-like movements of his brushes

mesmerized me as they moved this way and that across the paper, transforming the white surface into an amazing picture.

I loved to watch the water in the clear glass jar when he rinsed his brushes.

I am still captivated by the memory of the slow motion swirling, twisting, and turning of the colors dancing an ever-morphing ballet as his paint-laden brushes were gently dipped into the water.

Time seemed to have a different meaning as I stood there with him in his studio. It was amazing to watch a simple pencil sketch become an ink drawing and, almost like a time-lapse movie, a finished painting.

My father loved to draw and paint and he passed that passion on to me.

The tiny seed that was planted deep inside me when I was a little boy watching my dad paint has blossomed into a career for me. I have written and illustrated over fifty books and have participated in a number of art shows over the years.

Silently, my father and I formed a special creative bond that grew from mutual respect and unconditional love without a word being spoken.

Letting kids know what you consider your shortfalls helps you to connect with them. It also helps them see you as a human who understands what it is like to feel insecure or afraid.

Brené Brown says, "Being vulnerable while connecting with kids is a rich and fertile ground for teaching and cultivating a connection."

Joseph Chilton Pearce writes, "What we are teaches the child more than what we say, so we must be the way we want our children to become."

CHILDREN ARE DEPENDENT ON ADULTS FOR SURVIVAL AND SOMETIMES GO TO EXTREMES TO GET THE LOVE, NURTURING, AND CONNECTION THEY NEED

Most of the time, children who seek attention have a legitimate need. When kids cannot get a response from an adult, they can begin to feel desperate. This can lead to a fear of being abandoned. In this situation, children develop negative tactics to engage the adult. To the kids, being punished, yelled at, nagged, or sometimes even pushed away is better than being ignored. By bugging the adult or constantly being in their face, the child tries to make sure that they are not forgotten.

After a recent school talk, a young girl approached me and shared an experience she'd had with some bullies and how traumatic it had been for her.

I listened to the girl and gave her some tips in case it happened again.

Her school counselor came up to me afterward and said, "She's just looking for attention. Don't mind her. She's such a drama queen."

I was shocked at the counselor's comment. I believe that there is always some reason why a child seeks attention. Even if the girl was a so-called drama queen, there is usually something behind that kind of behavior.

I discovered afterward that the little girl's father was currently deployed and her mother was about to be separated from her stepfather, and the school counselor had no idea this was happening. It took me a few minutes of simply listening to figure out what the child was trying to express by being a so-called drama queen.

Kids feel connected when the adults react with interest, affection, and approval.

However, when children feel disconnected and can't get a response, they sometimes get desperate.

Some children just need more interaction than others. This can be especially challenging to a parent who, by nature, doesn't need as much connection as their child does.

From personal experience, I can tell you that getting into trouble by purposely acting out or being labeled a bad kid felt much better than being ignored by teachers at my school. By finding ways to push buttons, the child is in effect waving a red flag in front of the adult's face.

HOW TO RESPOND SO CHILDREN WILL HEAR

React as calmly as possible even if you are angry. Kids tend to tune out adults who appear frustrated, angry, or defensive.

Share your ideas and opinions without discounting theirs.

Resist arguing and instead frame your response in a neutral way, like "I know you don't agree with what I'm saying, but here's what I think."

Place attention on what the child may be feeling instead of reacting to your own feelings.

CONNECTING WITH WRITTEN WORDS

Journaling can be a very powerful connector. A great example of this is a note I got from a child who was going through a tough time while her father was deployed to Afghanistan. I encouraged her to write what she was feeling and to share those thoughts with her father.

Dear Mr. Trevor Romain,

My dad was deployed 3 times and I felt like he did not know us. I sometimes got so sad it hurt inside and I was real depressed because it felt like he was not my same dad. This time when he was deployed I wrote my feelings down in my journal like you told us. When my dad came home I showed him my journal and he cried and when he cried I knew he got his feelings back. And when he got his feelings back that's when I knew I got my daddy back.

—Delissa

By simply writing down what she was feeling, this little girl was able to reconnect with her father when he came home from the war.

SOMETIMES, CONNECTIONS ARE MADE WITHOUT YOU EVEN REALIZING IT

Like journaling, sending notes is a very effective way to connect when the conditions may not be favorable for a face-to-face connection.

I learned about using notes to connect when I was in the army. It happened the day I almost stabbed myself in the chest with a bayonet.

I was walking back to my tent after being issued my army equipment. It was the first day of basic training at the 4th Field Regiment Base in Potchefstroom.

We felt really proud, and rather important, as we walked back to our tents with our FN rifles in hand.

Some of us popped the bayonets onto the weapon

we were given, which made us feel even more important.

I was busy trying to figure out how to fit the bayonet onto the barrel when I spotted her.

There were hundreds of troops stationed there, but she was the only female soldier we had seen on the whole base. I think during my entire two years of national service, I only saw four or five women in uniform.

She was a lieutenant assigned to our regimental headquarters.

She was rather attractive, and I fell in love with her instantly. Along with a few hundred other depraved eighteen- and nineteen-year-old mongrels.

I was so busy looking at her, I tripped over the guide wire of our tent and almost impaled myself on my bayonet. As you would expect, the guys never let me forget that.

We caught glimpses of her all throughout basic training, and she even spoke to me once during that time. Actually, it wasn't really speaking; it was more like a grunt as I saluted her.

About six months later, I was sent to run what they called the media center in the headquarters. My job was to head up a team of guys to create diagrams on plastic sheets for overhead projectors. Officers used the sheets for lectures.

The rather pretty lieutenant worked in an office in the building.

I think I spent more time walking past her office and going to get a drink of water than doing my work.

I'm happy to say our relationship developed quite a lot after I started working in that building. By a lot, I mean she grunted at me daily when I saluted her. I don't think she said two words to me in the year that I worked there.

She had pretty, green-blue eyes. They were slightly different in color. She was a classic Afrikaans beauty. Intellectually, I knew that there was no chance on God's earth that she and I would ever be an item.

First, she was about ten years older than me.

Second, she was a career military officer, and I was a lowly lance bombardier doing my two years of national service.

Third, she was a tall, attractive, strong woman, and I was a short, scrawny, certified knucklehead.

But love is a funny thing. It will not listen to logic, and it will totally ignore reality.

Love makes people blithering idiots.

Love has a way of blocking out reality no matter how much you try not to let it.

Love has a tendency to become very dangerous when placed in the wrong hands. Hands like mine. Especially when there is a pen around, and a pen is how my obsession with the rather pretty lieutenant turned from fantasy into a potential disaster.

I honestly just meant to do it once. A small gesture, if you will. But things do not always turn out as planned.

The first note I dropped into the ceramic pencil holder on her desk was a little drawing I had done of a person smiling.

It was quite simple really. Her desk was right by the door, and it was quite easy to pop the note in there when nobody was watching.

The second note did not have any words either. In fact, none of the notes I ever delivered had writing on them because I never wanted to be identified. I can only imagine the consequences, never mind the ridicule, if the commandant had found out.

I felt pretty safe, though, because there were a number of guys who worked in the media center with me who could draw as well.

After a while, I started adding a little heart to each picture I drew.

What was I thinking? Apparently, I wasn't thinking, because, about once a week, I left her a little love drawing.

I don't know what I was expecting, but whatever it was, it didn't happen.

A few months later, the lieutenant was transferred back to the Army's Women's College.

I was saddened by the news.

Intellectually, I knew nothing would ever come of my illustrated love notes, but deep down inside, there had always been a little spark of hope, a fantasy that she would suddenly walk into my office, throw her arms around me, and tell me that my little notes had made her fall in love with me.

The commandant and his staff had a little goodbye party for the rather pretty lieutenant, and because of my lowly rank, I was not invited to the shindig.

I sat at my little desk, hoping to catch one last glimpse of her as she walked by our office for the last time.

I heard everyone wishing her well, and I looked up as she passed the door.

She did not even look in. She was carrying her personal belongings and was on her way out of my life forever.

Then, to my surprise and subsequent horror, she stepped back and looked into the office from the hallway.

"Romain!" she barked.

We all scrambled to our feet, which was army protocol when an officer entered a room.

"Cute pictures. Nice notes," she said with a slight smile. "Thank you."

Then she was gone.

"Cute pictures?" said one of the guys. "What is she talking about?"

"I have no idea," I said, shrugging. I wish I could have seen the look on my own face.

LAUGHTER IS A GREAT ICE BREAKER AND A GOOD CONNECTOR

The movie that inspired my career the most was *Patch Adams*. For those who haven't seen it, the story is about a man who commits himself to a mental institution because he is suicidal. While there, he learns that the doctors are not truly concerned for the well-being of their patients, which inspires him to enter the medical field with the revolutionary approach of using humor, empathy, and love instead of the clinical textbook approach.

Dr. Adams believes that patients should not be treated conventionally but psychologically and spiritually. He does this by making them feel love, laughter, friendship, and safety, in spite of whatever disease or condition they may be suffering from. He does this by dressing up as a clown and using humor to connect with patients.

By doing this, Dr. Hunter "Patch" Adams has changed the lives of thousands of people.

Being silly is one of the most powerful tools in my connector kit. I have connected with kids all over the world, no matter where they live and what situation they are in, by making a total idiot of myself.

This connection, inspired by Dr. "Patch" Adams, helps me to break the ice and create bonds with children under the most trying, difficult, and uncomfortable situations. I use self-deprecating humor, silly jokes, rhymes, and a few easy magic tricks to help me.

If a child lives with criticism, he learns to condemn.
If a child lives with hostility, she learns to fight.
If a child lives with ridicule, he learns to be shy.
If a child lives with fear, she learns to be apprehensive.
If a child lives with shame, he learns to feel guilty.
If a child lives with tolerance, she learns to be patient.
If a child lives with encouragement, he learns to be confident.

If a child lives with acceptance, she learns to love.

If a child lives with recognition, he learns to have goals.

If a child lives with honesty, she learns what truth is.

If a child lives with fairness, he learns justice.

If a child lives with security, she learns to have faith in herself.

If a child lives with friendliness, he learns to be kind, compassionate, and empathetic and how to get along in the world.

—Anonymous

You cannot have a real connection with a child if you are constantly glancing at your phone or tablet.

Kneeling down to the child's level, making eye contact, and even tilting your head shows the child that you are focusing on and listening to what they are telling you.

If connection is the energy that surges between people, we have to remember that those surges must travel in both directions.

—Brené Brown

A SIMPLE WAY TO CONNECT

A great way to help kids learn how to be spontaneous and communicate well is the bowl game. Make notes with the child's favorite topics and place them in a bowl. Ask the child to pick out a topic and speak about it for one minute. As time goes by, kids get more confident, comfortable, and enthusiastic about sharing information about what they love.

When talking to both kids and adults, I often ask myself if I am actually listening or just waiting to speak.

HOW TOTAL MISCOMMUNICATION WITH MY FATHER TAUGHT US BOTH HOW TO COMMUNICATE

Communication often disconnects when we assume that we are certain we know something about a child instead of inquiring about the child's truth.

Case in point. I was about six years old. My father took me fishing on the Vaal River in South Africa near my grandfather's farm. It was spring, and the leaves on the trees were a million shades of fresh green. We found a perfect spot under some willow trees on the riverbank.

I snooped around the immediate area while my father set up. When I got back from my exploring, I found everything ready. Two folding chairs were set up facing the lake. Two fishing rods were loaded and ready to go.

My father cast my line for me and rested the fishing pole on a Y-shaped twig he'd cut from one of the trees. "Now, don't take your eye off that pole," he said. "The minute it moves, you grab it and jerk it like I showed you."

He threw in his own line and rested it on another Y-shaped stick. Then he opened the newspaper and settled back into his chair. Within thirteen seconds, I was bored. I drew patterns on the sand around the chair with my shoes.

Then I leaned far back on my chair and tried to see if I could see any stars in the deep-blue sky. I knew the stars were there somewhere. Suddenly, I lost my balance and began falling backward. I paddled with my arms, trying not to fall. It seemed to take forever. I hit the ground hard and winded myself. For a second, I couldn't move. *I'm paralyzed*, I thought.

I looked at my dad, hoping he'd rush over and comfort me, tell me it was all right and that he'd love me even though I was handicapped. And he'd give me things to prove it. But he didn't move.

He lowered his newspaper slowly. "My boy, you've got to be very quiet when you're fishing," he said. Before he could lift the newspaper again, my line jerked so hard that it pulled the pole right off the stick and almost into the water.

My father jumped up and grabbed the line. My back healed instantly, and thanks to the marvels of nature, I was no longer a paraplegic. My father grabbed me by the collar and pulled me over towards him. "Here, reel it in," he said excitedly. "It's your first fish."

I was scared and elated. I grabbed the pole and clumsily reeled in the line, which got tighter and tighter until it was almost impossible to reel any more. Then I jerked the pole back, and suddenly the line gave.

I thought I'd lost the fish, but I'd actually pulled it right out of the water. It landed at my feet, flipping and jumping as it gasped for air.

I was horrified.

"Good boy!" yelled my father. "Now, put your foot on it, and let's get rid of the hook."

The fish looked at me. I knew it was scared. I raised my foot and placed it gently on the fish's body. The fish jerked away and then suddenly jumped towards me.

I screamed and ran. My father grabbed the fish and brought it over to me. It was squirming in his hand, mouth gaping. The hook had ripped through the inside of the fish's mouth and was sticking out of its cheek. I took two steps back.

"Let me show you," said my father, and he ripped the hook out of the fish's mouth. My stomach turned. I wanted to be sick.

He threw the fish into the ice chest and quickly closed the lid. "Well done," he said, sitting down and picking up the paper.

My father smiled, but not his normal smile – this one was made up for me.

He caught two more fish, one on his line and one on mine, which I refused to reel in.

Soon after he caught the last fish, we packed up and got ready to go home. Before we left, nature called, and my father disappeared into the bushes for a few minutes.

Wanting to take another look at the fish, I opened the chest and peeked in. All three were lying on the bottom, their silver scales glinting in the late-afternoon sun. I closed the chest and sat on it.

I gazed out at the river. It was a crimson-tinted

mirror in the setting sun. It was hard to believe that hundreds of fish were swimming around under that mirror. I wondered if our fish had brothers or sisters.

I stood up, opened the chest again, grabbed one of the fish, and ran down to the water's edge. I threw the fish as far as I possibly could. I watched it tumble through the air and shatter the river as it broke the surface. Then I ran back, grabbed the other two fish, and threw them into the water too.

"What was that?" said my father as he pushed through the bushes. I looked at the river without answering. He followed my gaze, his eyes finally resting on the three fish floating on the surface.

He didn't say anything.

He picked up the chairs and fishing rods and walked towards the car. "Do me a favor, my boy," he said over his shoulder. "Please go and rinse the chest in the river."

I took the chest down to the water. I dipped it into the river and scooped up some water. I stood up.

The fish were still floating on the surface. I picked up the chest and ran back up the bank towards my father. Just before we got to the trees, I turned and took one more look at the river.

A sudden movement caught my eye. There was a ripple around the fish. I held my breath. Slowly, one of the fish rolled over and, with a lazy flap of its fin, disappeared under the surface. Within a few seconds, the other fish followed. Then the ripples were gone, and the lake became a mirror again.

My dad came up behind me and rested his hand on my shoulder.

"You okay?" he said.

"I'm not sure," I replied truthfully, on the verge of tears. "I kind of feel bad."

"Feel bad for those fish, huh?" he said.

"No," I said. "I feel bad about disappointing you, Dad."

"Aw, buddy. You didn't disappoint me," he said, ruffling my hair. "I'm not that crazy about fishing myself. I actually hate taking the hook out of the fish's mouth. Ugh."

"Ugh," I repeated.

He put his arm around me, and we walked back to the car together.

After that, my father always asked me sincerely about things we did together, and I always answered him truthfully even if I thought it might hurt his feelings.

Children will sometimes disconnect because they are fearful of being wrong or making a mistake. What they don't realize is that we are all fearful of being wrong, of being belittled, of making mistakes.

Kids are not experienced enough to understand that making mistakes or being wrong builds courage and resilience. You can help a child stay connected during times like this by sitting in their own vulnerability with them and sharing stories of your own experiences on the subject.

THE BEST GIFT YOU CAN GIVE A CHILD IS BEING PRESENT

After my run a few days ago, I was stretching in a little park where the running trail ends.

A dad and his five- or six-year-old son were playing with a ball nearby. They were having so much fun. The look of absolute joy on the little boy's face was so heartwarming. Their connection was amazing.

It was great to see that the boy's father was one hundred percent present. All the time he was there, I never saw him once pull out a phone or even let his attention drift away from the boy.

At one point, the ball fell to the ground, and they both tumbled onto to the grass, wrestling for it.

When I replay the scene in my mind, for some reason, I see it in slow motion.

The smiles, the grins, the deep blue sky behind them, the boy's long, curly hair falling over his little face as they sweetly fought for the ball.

The love between them was palpable.

Still in slow motion, I saw the dad grab the ball, jump to his feet, and begin to run from the boy.

After a few steps, his feet seemed to get tangled up, and I watched him fall hard to the ground.

For a few seconds, he just lay motionless on his back, arms splayed by his sides.

The boy, who was curled up in a ball when his father took off, looked up and saw his dad lying on the grass.

The look of concern on the little boy's face is frozen in my mind like a Time Life black and white photograph.

In a panic, the boy got up and ran over to his dad.

I could hear him asking his father if he was all right.

The man reached up, pulled the boy to the ground, and rolled around, hugging him.

"I'm fine," he said, chuckling and tickling the boy. "I tripped on my own feet. That's what happens when you get older."

They both got up and walked away from me, toward the swings.

As they moved off, I could not fully hear their conversation, but I did hear the boy say, "Please don't die for a long time, Daddy. Okay?"

"I promise I'll try my best," said the dad.

"For reals?" said the boy.

"For reals," said the dad, ruffling the boy's hair.

As I turned to leave, I saw the dad put his arm around the boy's shoulder and pull him closer. The boy reciprocated, putting his arm around his dad's waist. Connected, they walked away.

HOW A SILLY PHRASE CONNECTED ME TO MY MOTHER DURING ONE OF THE TOUGHEST TIMES IN MY LIFE

Creating a ritual or a tradition is a powerful way to connect.

The Book of New Family Traditions tells the story of a family that had the tradition of squeezing each other's hands three times to signal the three words "I love you." On the day the daughter got married, the father squeezed her hand three times as he walked her down the aisle. Only she knew that this was happening, a tiny personal connection during an overwhelming and emotion-filled time. She said it was one of the most moving and connecting moments of her life.

Kids feel a special bond with a person when they have a secret handshake or a phrase that means something to both.

I was very close to my mother as a young child. We had a silly little phrase we shared whenever anything seemed insurmountable. If I had a scrape or a bump on my head or if I was worried about something, she would say, "Don't worry, it will go over." (We got that phrase from my Lithuanian grandmother.) When my mom was sad or upset, I would say the same to her: "It will go over." My mother is in her early eighties, and we still connect with that phrase.

Although it was a silly phrase, it was a powerful connector between my mother and me, especially when I was sick.

I remember one night, as a child, when I had a dangerously high fever that caused severe nosebleeds (and kept me in a pool of sweat for days). It seemed to take great pleasure in creating horrific, swirling hallucinations that scared me and made me mumble incoherently.

During that time, I woke up one night with an extremely high fever and felt so awful that I thought I was actually dying. My throat was parched, and I had a terrible headache from dehydration.

I frantically screamed for my mother from deep within my soul, but all my mouth could do was groan. (I still have nightmares of trying to scream but no voice coming out.)

My parents were just a few rooms away, and I wanted my mom to hold me because I didn't want to die by myself.

I was petrified because I was trying desperately to cry out to my parents but they could not hear me groaning due to the terrific Transvaal thunderstorm that was brewing outside.

The fever rendered me so lame that I could not even drag myself out of bed.

It was an awful feeling.

The wind was wrestling with the bushes outside my window, and the corresponding shadows on the wall looked like creatures from hell coming to take my life.

I squeezed my eyes shut, trying to get the images away.

Suddenly, I knew something was in my room. I could just feel it.

I opened my eyes in a panic.

A shadow moved away from the wall and loomed over me.

I heard a soft whisper that mingled with the leaves rustling outside.

I could not hear what the voice said.

I did not want to hear what the voice said.

It was a hissing whisper, and I was too afraid. But the whisper came closer and closer, and suddenly, I could hear it clearly in my ear.

"It's okay. It's okay, my boy. I'm here."

It was my mother.

I suddenly felt a cool cloth on my forehead and a glass of cold water in my hand.

I sipped the refreshing water, letting it soothe the fire in my throat.

My mom fluffed the pillows, straightened the sheets, and took the glass of water and placed it on the bedside table.

Then she did the sweetest thing. She climbed onto the bed and put her arms around me.

And lay with me.

And comforted me.

"It will go over," she whispered in my ear. "It will go over."

My mom was sleeping next to me when I woke up to a deep blue Johannesburg sky outside my window. Her face was so sweet and caring, and she looked so peaceful in her sleep.

I wanted my heart to be bigger so I could love her more.

Instead, I cuddled in closer to my ma and gently closed my eyes, knowing everything was going to go over and be okay.

And it was.

A CONNECTION WITH A CHILD THAT HELPED FORMULATE THE MEANING OF MY LFE

A brief connection I once had as a young man turned out to be completely life-changing and taught me the power of hope. It was initiated by a little African child in South Africa.

It happened while I was in the army. One second, I was your average South African soldier doing my national service. The next moment, I was your average South African soldier doing my national service, but I was different. I was different, but I didn't know it at the time.

My life didn't change because I went out of my

mind in the army or anything, although we were all a bit crazy, mainly from eating horrible food.

It wasn't because of being broken down and rebuilt the army way. Or from being bored out of our skulls. Or standing guard instead of having a weekend pass because some fool called his rifle a gun.

It wasn't because of a near-death experience when an idiot almost killed us at the shooting range because his rifle jammed and he was waving the weapon around trying to unjam the thing.

It wasn't because we had to bite the edges of our beds to make them square, or iron a seam in our shirts, or polish our boots in the dust for hours, or sleep on the floor so our beds could be perfect for the morning inspection.

No. None of that.

It was a simple connection. I've come to realize now that I'm a bit older that simple things are sometimes the most powerful life changers.

I did not wake up that morning with a premonition. I didn't have a dream that my life would change. It just happened naturally.

I was visiting a friend at the base, and for some

reason, on my way to my friend's room, I passed through the children's ward. There, I saw a little African kid sitting on the edge of one of the beds. He was about three or four years old. They said he was from the border between South West Africa (now Namibia) and Angola. The little boy's legs had been badly damaged in a landmine incident.

For some reason that I cannot explain, I was drawn to the kid. That's where it all started.

Literally.

I walked over to him, and he put his arms up to me. I didn't know what to do. I looked around. No nurses or doctors were in the ward, only an old man cleaning the floor with a mop, but he didn't seem particularly interested in the kid.

What happened next is why I now work with kids who are terminally ill, hurting in some way, or who have suffered trauma.

The boy whimpered and reached out to me. Without giving it a second thought, I bent down and picked him up. He put his arms around me.

I have never been held so tightly in my life. He hugged me and wouldn't let go. The connection was electric and palpable. He put his little face against my neck and started to cry.

His tears ran down my neck.

And inside my shirt.

And touched my heart.

And changed my world.

Not changed as in "Ahaaaa, I now know the meaning of life." Not changed in the biblical sense. Not changed as in "Stand back, people – now I know my mission."

To tell the truth, I did not even know that my life had changed at the time except that as I was hitching back to base a few days later, I kept on thinking about that little kid and his sad little face buried in my neck. I had no clue it was happening, but in the deepest part of my soul, a small micro-seed of compassion had started to grow.

Connecting with the little boy that day set off a little spark deep inside me, one that became the light that now guides me, especially when I get lost in the darkness of my own self-importance.

CONNECTING THROUGH VISUALIZATION

During a school visit in Germany, on one of our tours, a mother of one of the kids approached me and asked if I would speak to her child. He was about twelve years old and extremely angry and frustrated. He was having bully problems, and he had moved to multiple schools because his dad was in the military and was currently deployed. The boy was not interested in talking at all. I asked him if he was angry. He nodded.

"Okay," I said. "You don't have to talk to me, but do me a favor, okay?"

He nodded again.

"Great. Sit down. Now, I want you to place both your feet firmly on the ground. Now, I want you to close your eyes. Imagine there is a volcano of anger rumbling at your feet. All the anger and frustration you have is brewing at your feet. Feel it."

He nodded once more.

"Now, I want you to imagine that the energy and anger and frustration is flowing up your legs and into your thighs. Feel it boiling in your stomach. Then visualize it moving powerfully through your chest and up through your neck, and with a big push, let it burst out of the top of your head."

The boy opened his eyes.

"I'm not sure," he said.

"Let's do it once more," I urged, "but try your best this time to fully imagine that your anger is a volcano inside of you that you are pushing out of the top of your head."

"Okay," he said.

"Go for it," I replied.

He closed his eyes and followed my instructions.

As I reached the end, I said loudly, "Now, blow that yucky stuff inside you right out of the top of your head as hard as you can. Get rid of it right now."

The boy clenched his fists and grunted, "Uggghh!" Then he opened his eyes and said, "Wow. It worked."

His mother, who was sitting off to the side, was beside herself with joy.

The boy and I sat together for almost thirty minutes after that discussing his anger and frustration.

Visualization is a powerful tool and, as in this case, a great way to connect with kids.

NEVER UNDERESTIMATE THE POWER OF YOUR WORDS

Sometimes, just a few words spoken in jest or in a shaming or demeaning way can stay with kids for the rest of their lives.

At school, due to my ADD, I was told I was an idiot and not very smart. I believed that until I was almost thirty years old, when I realized that I'm actually not an idiot.

Words have incredible power. An example of this is the shortest novel in the world, attributed to Ernest Hemingway. Here it is in its entirety:

Baby shoes. For sale. Never worn.

This may be the end of the book, but certainly not the end of my mission and quest to help adults connect with kids, even in the most trying situations.

I will continue sharing information, research, anecdotes, and stories at www.trevorromain.com. Please join me there.